Baby Steps

SECRETS OF A

MILLIONAIRE

Achieve Financial Freedom Without Stress

BY

JOHN DEREL

CONTENTS

CHAPTER

1

Introduction
Why you Should Become a Millionaire?

Reaching the million-dollar mark is a difficult task which is achieved by those willing to put in the required effort. If you are looking for a **quick way** to make a million dollars, you might be disappointed. Becoming a millionaire requires a high level of risk, which yields a high level of reward.

Although becoming a millionaire is now easier than ever, few people are willing to follow the steps involved. Many 'play it safe' or give in to procrastination.

The Baby steps secrets of Becoming a millionaire is not about spending a million dollars, it's about earning millions.

The following are seven reasons why you should become a millionaire:

1. **Make an Impact:** when you are a millionaire, it is easier to help others. Being wealthy empowers others to follow the same path. Money is constantly flowing when you are tipping a server or purchasing goods or services.

Since a millionaire pays more taxes than others, the government can fund basic services such as roads, schools, libraries, and law enforcement. Millionaires in the United States pay nearly 40% of their income in taxes. If you make a million dollars in a year, you have made over $400,000. This amount of money has a far greater societal impact than the $15,000 average contribution made by most taxpayers.

2. **Inspire Others:**

You can inspire others. What most wealthy people do behind the scenes inspires others. When there is more money, you can work on projects that are more meaningful and devote more time to charitable endeavours.

You more choices, and control over your life.

3. Absolute control

There are two types of individuals: Those who try fit their lifestyles into their wages and those who set their wages and create the lifestyles they desire. Unfortunately, over 90% of the world's population work for money. They allow money take control of their lives.

Do not spend 50 hours or more in a job you hate.

4. Money provides freedom in life. One of the greatest benefits of wealth is the ability to enjoy your money. You enjoy luxuries you had no idea existed!

Furthermore, when you are a millionaire, you can do whatever you want, with whom you want, whenever you want.

5. **You can Accomplish More**. When there is money, you have the impression that you can accomplish almost anything. Money does not raise your self-esteem, but it does allow you to think more clearly and be yourself.

You'll have "peace of mind." The average person has little to no life insurance, which means that when he or she passes away, there will be no money left for the family to cover funeral costs and other expenses. A $10,000,000 policy, is better than having a $0 policy.

6. **Philanthropy:** You can give back in many ways. Most people have no idea where their money is going or why it is going there. They write checks out of a sense of "guilt" or "shame." When you reach the million mark, giving to causes you care about becomes easy.

You have a choice in terms of how you give. You have the option of giving your money on a general or specific basis. Furthermore, giving can be enjoyable and can be done in a variety of ways. You can bless more people with money. Giving is the key to living.

7. **An Exciting Journey:**

Becoming a millionaire it takes you through an exciting journey filled with twists, turns, and upheaval. However, if you endure, you'll discover that it was worth it.

"If you don't figure out how to make money while you sleep, you'll keep working until you die."

Warren Buffett

"The greatest risk is not taking any risk at all." In a rapidly changing environment, failure is guaranteed when we avoid taking risks." Mark Zuckerburg

CHAPTER

2

The baby Steps Begin.

Try to be the first one in and the last one out. Will it affect your social life? Yes, a little bit.

I started working by 5:30 a.m. and closed at 7:30 p.m. I became knowledgeable, accomplished more, and received the respect of my peers. In addition, my boss's recognizes my work ethic, which allowed me keep my position.

2. **Take a Balanced Approach.**

Investing in an S & P 500 index fund is OK, but Avoid going insane and squandering all your money. With $4,000 to invest when I was 22, I placed 80% of my money in a single stock and earned a 5,000% return. A portion of it was fortunate. However, I conducted research, took a significant risk, and it paid off.

Buy Real Estate.

Make it a goal to choose a place to live for the next five to ten years. Make it a goal to invest in properties. If you make a 20% down payment on a property and the value increases by 3% every year, you will get a 15% return on your investment.

4. **Become frugal with spending.**

Young people love Spending money on things they don't need to impress their peers or post on social media.

There is no stigma attached to being young and impoverished. Avoid eating out daily. Avoid buying clothes you do not need - thanks to Mark Zuckerberg and Steve Jobs, wearing the same thing every day is cool. Be the low-key millionaire next door.

I got a six-year-old automobile and drove it for the next ten years after becoming a millionaire. Following that, I rented and drove a Honda Fit for three years. I still dress in the same casual athletic attire that I did in my twenties.

7. **Start a Side Business**

Earn money by working a full-time job or establishing your own company. Even better, you can combine the two. With time, your

side hustle may grow into a large company that earns more than your full-time work.

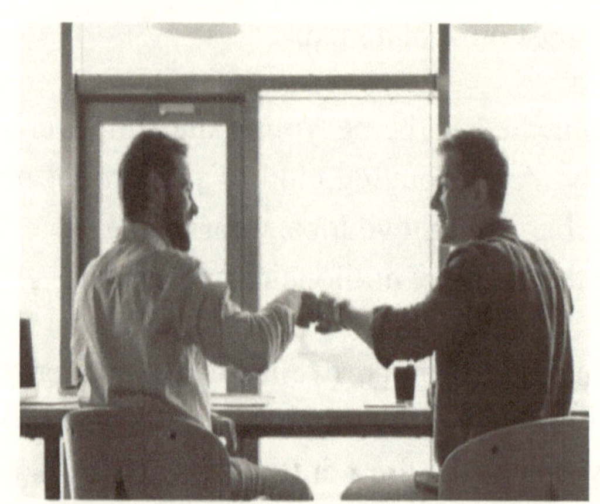

8. **Make quality friends .**

Make as many friends as possible. Being a diligent worker is enough. Engage in quality conversation with others.

Once you have the support of someone with authority, your whole career will improve significantly. I made it a point to take a co-worker out for coffee every week. Developing strong contacts aided in my promotion to vice president at the age of 27.

Invest in your education.

Your mind is your most valuable asset. A solid education is the most precious asset you have, so continue to broaden your horizons, even after college. Thanks to the Internet, you can now learn practically anything free.

When I completed my part-time MBA degree, I continued to take courses to keep current on all things finance-related

Keep a record of your progress.

Use the free financial tools available online. Maintain control of your money by tracking your cash flow, analyzing your investment portfolio, and calculating your retirement financial requirements.

CHAPTER

3

Self-Confidence Steps

Many Successful entrepreneur struggle with self-doubt while trying new business ideas. What distinguishes them is that they never allow such emotions to slow them down.

You need self-confidence, which is not difficult to get.

We are born into a world filled with anxiety and insecurity. Confidence is something that you get by tackling the obstacles holding you back.

Steps To Building Your Confidence:

1. Recognize when self-doubt arises.

Rather than dwelling on self-doubt and blaming yourself for it, just recognize it for what it is and let it pass.

2. Learn from Past Successes and Failures.

When Steve Blank debuted on the cover of wired magazine in 1994, they thought his business, Rocket Science Games, would transform the video gaming industry. Three months later, he found himself facing the loss of $35 million in investor investment and a certain collapse.

Use the failures to propel yourself ahead. If any situation brings opportunity to learn, Focus on them and note the lessons that may be learned.

3. Go beyond your comfort zone.

Attempt new things as often as possible.

New challenges will overcome fear. You will discover how resilient you are in the face of adversity.

Start with simple tasks. For example, taking up an activity that you love, e.g. scuba diving, learning a new dance, programming an app, or refining your jump shot.

4. Find a Mentor

Do not overlook the benefit of having someone to confide in. A mentor has experience; they have "been there, done that." They can readily point out potential problems, ensuring that you avoid making the same errors. When these mentors lighten your path, you will grow in confidence.

5. Learn to Say "No"

It is natural trying to satisfy others, especially when you are seeking contacts, networking, pleasing possible investors, and making those early entrepreneurial choices. However, saying "yes" to everyone will stress you in more ways than you can manage. This will result in stress, maybe sadness, and even burnout, all of which will occur before you get an opportunity to launch.

Saying 'No' shows you value your own time and resources and compels others to do the same.

6. Develop A Change Strategy.

Confidence is built with practice. It is earned through diligence. Confident individuals are self-aware, and the genuine confidence they possess is rooted firmly in the world they have constructed. If you want to improve, you must conduct an honest and accurate self-evaluation of your talents. Pay attention to the voice that informs you of your limitations and then seek to enhance those abilities.

Ignoring your mistakes won't make them disappear. You must devise strategies to mitigate their harmful influence. As a result, you'll have a clear grasp of your talents and how you can use them to develop as a result.

Self-confidence makes it easier to dismiss unjustified feedback, criticism, and self-doubt.

CHAPTER

4

The Millionaire Mindset

Our minds are weapons which when used effectively, has a great impact on your life. Your focus in life will grow and become significant to you.

The more you focus and concentrate, the more it develops and expand. Dwelling on your previous failures, makes them seem bigger and a burden to carry. On the other hand, if you focus on your accomplishments, you feel fulfilled.

Your mentality shapes your reality. If you see the world as a nasty, unpleasant place, it will affect your perception of reality.

When your reality is giving and helpful, you are empowered to achieve. Earl Nightingale said, ***"We become what we think about most of the time."***

The millionaire mentality focuses on allowing and equipping you to act following your convictions without making excuses.

Know What It Takes, What It Takes, Never Give Up, and Focus, Focus, Focus.

Being wealthy requires determination, bravery, knowledge, competence, 100% of your work, a never-say-die mentality, and, of course, a wealthy mind.

Thinking like a millionaire requires focus.

Although things may not always go according to plan, and some decisions might not seem ideal, millionaires rise more often than they fall, and they continue pushing toward their final goal.

the right attitude is important to go through difficulties and achieve your objectives.

Steps to a Millionaire Mindset

1. Have a vision.

If you set a goal to be a millionaire or start a seven-figure business at some point in your life, know the reason why you want it. Making more money was my "why" throughout my twenties.

You must be clear on your "why" so that when circumstances become rough or you will not feel like waking up at 4 a.m. or making another cold call, you are compelled to do so.

What kind of impact do you want to make? What are the benefits of accomplishing your seven-figure objective, and even more compelling, what are the disadvantages of failing to achieve it? When we make our vision and "why" about others, the inspired action we take to attain it increases exponentially.

Stop procrastination, and take action immediately, despite how frightening or difficult it may seem. Understanding the why and being a "now" person can motivate you to achieve your goals.

2. Be Passionate.

Speak life into your current circumstances and alter your perspective such that you value your employment as it allows you to pursue the career you love.

3. Be Solution-oriented.

Being solution-focused means that, regardless of your circumstances, you find solutions where others perceive problems. Thus, when the going gets tough and most people pack up and go home, the millionaire mind understands that there is always a solution and that every issue or obstacle, no matter how large, is a gift in disguise. Even failure has some advantages that will assist you in the future.

By focusing on solutions rather than problems, you develop a good attitude and avoid being thrown off track by situations beyond your control.

CHAPTER

5

Budgeting day by day

If you have been putting it off for a long time because you think budgets are not necessary or they do not work, think again.

Budgets are boring, restricting, and tell you what you cannot have.

Budgets can help you save money, pay off your debts as times change, and people change.

Plain, simple, and effective budgeting are what I do.

In its most basic form, a living budget is a plan for how much money you have coming in and how you plan to spend it each month.

Being frugal means sticking to your budget so you do not go overboard and never run out of money for the month.

You also have funds set aside for future expenses.

You can make several different types of budgets.

Mine is loosely based on the zero budgeting method, which simply means that you'll budget all of your money and assign each dollar a task until there's nothing left.

Then there is the 50/30/20 spending plan.

If you are unfamiliar with the 50/30/20 budget, it states that you should spend 50% of your income on necessities, 30% on wants, and 20% on savings.

This budget does not appeal to me.

The issue I have with it is that it assumes you can meet all of your needs with only half of your income!

In my opinion, spending 30% of your income on wants is extravagant.

If you start saving in your early twenties and continue to do so throughout your working life, 20% is a good figure to aim for.

Budgeting has many advantages. Try getting more out of your budget.

The following are some of the advantages of budgeting:

You are less likely to get into debt because you know exactly how much money you have. There aren't any costs to throw your finances off.

When your budget is a little tight overall, you look for ways to save (if this is you, I strongly suggest you start with your grocery budget; there is always wiggle room there).

Because you know where your money is going, you are in a much

better position to achieve your financial goals.

Worrying about money during the night is no longer an issue.

Budgeting Money On A Budget

I believe that budgeting is critical when you have a low income since every penny earned must be put to good use .

Some necessary expenses includes rent and utility bills, while others are more flexible and discretionary.

You have options when it comes to how and what you spend this money. Taking out a new car loan or overspending on your credit card are considered necessary spending because a decision has been made, and decisions must be paid for.

Before you get your bills or calculator out, think about what you want.

Set Goals

Goals are what you aspire to or willing to go for. They are the reason for having a budget in the first place. Your objectives might look like this:

- Pay off your debts.

- Start putting money aside for your retirement.

- Put money aside for a vacation.

Make your goals specific, such as paying off $200 in debt each month instead of just paying off debt.

As a result, the above objectives become something like this:

Each month, pay off $200 in debt.

Start putting aside $100 per month for retirement.

Every month, set aside $50 for a vacation.

These are just a few examples . I'm not suggesting that saving $100 a month for retirement is sufficient, nor that $50 will get you very far on a family vacation. But if that's all you've got this month, go ahead and set those goals.

You can increase these figures in the future.

Keep in mind that goals equal necessary spending.

On an old-fashioned cash register, there's a $1 button in red to show how to budget money.

The First Step

Firstly, find out how much money you have coming in each month.

This will include your wages, side hustle earnings, any benefits you may receive (for example, child benefits in the United Kingdom), and any bank interest on any savings you may have.

So you know the maximum amount of money you can spend right now, not a penny more.

Step 2 of the process

List your expenses and how much each one costs. Pull out your bills and check your bank and credit card statements to find this information.

Your automated bills will appear on your statements. Add them to the bills you have pulled out to pay by hand. Some examples of basic expenses is your rent or mortgage.

- Bills for utilities (of course, you can reduce how much you have to pay by careful use of your electricity, gas, and water)
- Payments on the loan have already been established (longer term, you will want to get rid of these and save up to pay cash for big-ticket items).
- Insurance policies (house, car, medical)

The following items will be included in non-essential spending:

- Food

- The cost of travel

- Clothing

- Cable/TV package

- Entertainment

- Going out to eat

- Holidays

- Education

- Beauty/grooming

- Gifts

- Taken out and spent cash

- And, without a doubt, many other things!

Some of these may appear to be necessities on the surface, but the amount of money spent on each of them is highly variable and unique to each of us.

On a white background, a patterned pink old-fashioned clip purse with coins spilling out.

Loan payments do not last indefinitely.

Once the loan is paid off, you will have more money to plan with and to help you achieve your financial objectives.

How much of your income is spent on bills?

When I was in my twenties, my bills, especially the essential ones in this first category, probably accounted for about 80% of my income. With no mortgage, no loans, and no childcare expenses, my essential bills now account for a much smaller percentage of my income.

I'm getting less money in, but I'm also getting less money out.

Step 3 of the process

This involves calculating how much money you have left after you've budgeted and paid for your necessary expenses.

Simply subtract your necessary expenses from your total income for this step.

Step 4

Now write down all of your other monthly expenses, but do not assign a dollar amount to them just yet.

On your bank and credit card statements, you can see how much you spent.

Even if you cannot recall how you spent the cash you drew from ATMs, make sure you include it.

This is non-essential spending, meaning it does not fall into the above-mentioned essentials category

You could live off rice and beans every day and save a bundle on groceries (I do not recommend it!).

When money is tight, here is how to make the most of a $35/£30 grocery budget for two people.

Clothing

Go to a charity shop or a thrift store to get cheap clothes.

This includes everything you ever spend money on that is not on your much smaller essentials list, your non-essential spending list should be quite long.

Step 5 of the Budgeting Process

You cannot spend more than you earn each month.

For some reason, none of us ever has enough money in our budget to cover everything we want. You will discover that the money you have coming in is insufficient for what you think you want. If you are currently paying $400 in-car payments or loan repayments, that is $400 you could be spending on something else once those loans are paid off.

Step 6 of the budgeting process

Your spending plan should now look like this:

Total income = X

Y = essentials, Z = non-essentials

X–Y–Z = 0

Congratulations! You now have a working budget that is alive and frugal. You should decide how much you want to spend your money.

Now you are in charge of making decisions, and as you can see, you have a many options.

You won't have any regrets if you stick to your budget.

Budgeting for the Future

As the months pass, your debt will decrease, and your budget should be adjusted.

Keep the money in a separate account and is replenished monthly. When an unexpected bill arrives, you pay it with the funds in that account.

As a result, a sinking fund category should be included in your budget. Keeping Track of Your Spending

They say, "Education, education, education." Education assists you in making well-informed decisions. Use the data to create a monthly budget plan that is tailored to your specific needs.

How do you go about doing this?

By keeping track of your expenditures, if you want to be more formal, you can say:

You should keep track of everything you spend so you can see where your money is going.

Keeping track of what you spend allows you to develop a more detailed picture of your spending habits and is often quite revealing.

Your tracker, on the other hand, will leave you with nowhere to hide!

You can keep track of your spending in a variety of ways to suit your needs. Do your budgeting on paper, in Excel, or even with a budgeting app. I

It's not about how you track things; it's about what you track.

Make a list of everything you spend money on. Do it daily if possible. At the very least, once a week.

And go over it once a month to see what you're spending and habits are saying.

Mine was a bit of a shocker, to say the least!

CHAPTER

6

Keeping a Rainy-Day Savings

A rainy day savings will pay for the unexpected bills that are not covered in your regular budget.

A rainy day fund is a money set aside for small out-of-pocket expenses that are not part of your regular living expenses. A rainy day fund is a one-time expense such as a car or home repairs.

You will feel better knowing that you can cover a few unexpected expenses. Also, it can be paid for without using your credit card or taking out a personal loan, both of which come with high-interest rates. Having a rainy day fund can also help you develop financial discipline.

What is the purpose of a rainy day fund?

To have a financial backup to accommodate unexpected expenses. You may not expect a thunderstorm or a broken washing machine, but both can occur at any time, so it's best to be ready.

How much money should I Keep?

It varies by person, but experts recommend starting with $1,000. For example, $1,000 should be enough to cover a minor car repair or a new appliance.

Your rainy day fund ideally should be equal to the maximum amount you can expect to pay for an unexpected bill. If your healthcare deductible is $1,500, you should set aside at least that amount in your emergency fund. The cost of car repairs varies, but common repairs such as brakes or alternators cost between $400 and $700. It is a good idea to increase your savings goal in case two rainy days occur close together.

Emergency Funds vs. Rainy Day Funds

An emergency fund is a larger financial safety net, typically three to six months' worth of living expenses. While a rainy day fund is typically smaller than an emergency fund, both are essential components of your financial strategy.

You can cover the extra costs without suffering too much hardship if you have funds set aside for non-routine expenses. If you don't have an emergency or rainy day fund, you might need to take out a personal loan or a payday loan. These loans have high-interest rates, which means you'll end up paying a lot more in the long run. Otherwise, you may find yourself taking money out of your 401(k) and other savings accounts, jeopardizing your long-term financial goals. You'll have peace of mind knowing you can cover any unexpected expenses if you have backup funds on hand.

How to Put Money Aside for a Rainy Day

There are several ways to build a rainy day fund, but the first step should be to create a budget or modify your current plan to include a rainy day fund contribution. This allows you to maximize your contribution until you reach your goal, after which you can divert that money to other savings accounts.

Here are some of the best ways to put money aside for a rainy day:

Create a direct deposit account: Make a separate direct deposit for your rainy-day fund so that a portion of your paycheck goes to it.

Make a monthly cash transfer: Set up an automatic transfer once a month. For instance, you might want to transfer $50 from your bank account to a money market fund once a month.

Put your spare change in a jar or piggy bank to start a rainy day fund. Your fund will begin small, but it will grow over time and will be easy to access.

Reduce your unexpected spending: If you normally have a latte in the morning or shop for new clothes once a month, consider reducing your spending for a few months. Put that extra cash in your rainy-day fund until you reach your target.

Where Should My Rainy Day Fund Be Invested?

Your rainy-day funds should be accessible and kept in a liquid account, which means you can access them quickly and without incurring fees. Money market accounts, savings accounts, and high-yield bank accounts are all excellent choices.

Your rainy day fund is separate from your other investments and keeps your finances organized. You will know exactly how much money you have and can access it when you need it.

It gives you financial security and peace of mind. When dark clouds appear, you will have a backup to cover expenses without having to take out a loan. You will become good at saving, which will open up new financial possibilities for you. With more money on hand, you can brighten up your future rainy days.

Keeping an Emergency Fund

Firstly, determine the amount to keep aside. It can be three months' worth of living expenses. Others may commit to six months. The most important thing to remember is that you have something in your emergency fund. Then you can gradually work toward your goal.

The same holds for your rainy day fund. Determine how much money you want in your fund and work backward from there. Divide the amount needed to adequately fund your account by the amount you can afford to save each month. Then you will have to figure out how many months it will take you to achieve your goal.

For example, your monthly expenses is $3,000 and you want to create a three-month emergency fund. That means you will need to set aside about $9,000 in your savings account. If you put aside $500 per month, your emergency fund is funded in about 18 months. While this may seem like a long time, keep in mind that unexpected windfalls such as tax returns, cash gifts, or even monetary inheritances can happen at any time. You can put some of this towards padding your emergency fund and reducing the time, it takes to fully fund it.

How much do you need?

The next step is to figure out how much money you'll need for a rainy day fund. In this case, considering some of your anticipated expenditures over the long term will assist you in determining how much you require. Do you own a senior pet? Do your children require braces? Do you live in a hurricane-prone or tornado-prone area? Is your air conditioner giving you trouble? Take all of this into consideration when making your decision.

Then, just like your emergency fund, divide the total by the amount you can spare each month. So, if you want a $2,000 rainy day fund and can save $75 per month, it will take you just over 27 months to reach your goal. You could also make other small budget cuts or collect spare change to contribute to your rainy day fund.

CHAPTER

7

Credit Card Debt Management

Managing your creditcard debt effectively might seem difficult. However, creditcard debt can be reduced and possibly eliminated with proper budgeting (including responsible spending), attention to due dates, having (and sticking to) a strategy, and paying more than the minimum due.

The Federal Reserve reported in June that revolving balances fell by 65 percent to $1.02 trillion in March and April, the largest drop in the report's 52-year history, wiping out two years of debt accumulation. Perhaps we followed the advice of personal finance experts and used federal Cares Act funds to pay down debt.

Consumers' average credit card debt was $6,354 at the same time that overall debt was falling. The average debt for consumers with balances (58 percent of all active card accounts) was a staggering $9,333.

Getting out of creditcard debt usually requires an approach that includes curbing spending, improving saving habits, and committing to a debt-reduction strategy. Creditcard balances had an average interest rate of 16.01 percent in June. That's a favourable rate, but it's huge since the Federal Reserve plans to keep lending rates to banks near zero until 2022; 30-year mortgage rates are hovering around 3%, and unsecured personal loans start at around 6%.

Like most people, paying off nearly $10,000 in credit card debt at a 16 percent interest rate will put your ability to buy a house, save for college, build a retirement nest egg, invest, or even deal with day-to-day expenses in jeopardy.

Credit Card Spending Habits in the United States

In 2021, the seven largest credit card issuers generated $3.517 trillion in purchase volume, a 25.6 percent increase. They accounted for 77.1 percent of the industry's total of $4.564 trillion.

The following is a breakdown of purchase volume from the top issuers of general-purpose credit cards in the United States, according to the 2022 Nilson Report

$950 billion for Chase
$868 billion for American Express
Citigroup: $483 billion

$455 billion for Capital One
Bank of America has a $414 billion market capitalization.
$182 billion was discovered.
$166 billion for a U.S. bank

Credit card holders spend more on items, check out with larger baskets, and focus on and remember more product benefits rather than costs.

According to the report "Neural Mechanisms of Credit Card Spending,"16 studies show that shoppers who use credit cards spend more on items, check out with larger baskets, focus on and remember more product benefits rather than costs, and make more indulgent and unplanned purchase choices.

The average household credit card debt is $8,590.

According to Wallethub, the average credit card debt per household in the United States is $8,590 as of Q4 2021.
As of 2019, credit card debt was the most commonly held type of debt.

According to the Federal Reserve, credit card debt was the most commonly held type of debt in 2019, with more than 45 percent of families reporting a credit card balance after their last payment.
 Americans in the 90th to 100th annual income percentile owed an average of $12,600 on credit cards.
When creditcard debt is broken down by household income, the higher the household income, the greater the credit card debt. Americans in the 90th to 100th annual income percentile

owed an average of $12,600.8 on credit cards.

Make timely payments on your credit card bills.

When you start your debt-reduction strategy, your main goal should be clear: On-time payment is essential. It's not just a few of your credit card bills, and it's not just Most of the time. Every single bill, all of the time.

Your creditcard agreement's fine print (which you probably didn't read) gives the issuer plenty of ammunition to make your financial life a living hell with a single late payment. Card issuers can hit you with late fees, higher interest rates, and credit-limit reductions in addition to damaging your credit score with reports to the Big Three (Experian, Trans-America, and Equifax).

Learn to live within your means and keep an eye out for ways to save money.

This starts with a review of your current earnings and spending patterns. You may also make changes; and reduce your spending.

Avoid Impulse Purchases — A few impulse purchases per month can easily derail a budget.

 Reduce your extravagances - Instead of going to the coffee shop, bring your mug. Do not let magazine covers, pop-up ads, or storefronts pique your interest in fashion.

Look for Bargains.

 At the grocery store, look for less expensive store brands.

Next, post reminders of your ultimate goal in prominent locations. The children's ideal college when you are tempted to change, confronting the bigger goal can help you stay on track.

Paying more than the minimum is one of the most effective strategies, as is the debt snowball, debt avalanche, and automation. Paying more than the bare minimum involves just that. Below is more information on this strategy.

The **debt snowball method** involves paying off the smallest balance first (and keeping it paid off), then rolling the money saved into the next smallest balance, motivated by your sense of accomplishment. As your confidence grows, so does the amount you can apply to each successive debt balance, until you're paying off your debt with larger and larger payments, like a snowball rolling down a hill.

The **debt avalanche** is a dubious name for a debt snowball variation. Rather than going after the lowest balance, you go after the one with the highest interest rate. The debt avalanche compensates for its lack of instant gratification by being more cost-effective and paying off credit card debt faster.

Automating your payments is an easy way to ensure that you pay your bills on time, avoiding late fees, penalty interest, and negative credit reports. If you are going for the snowball or avalanche strategy, be aware of your debts' shifting nature. Also, keep a close eye on your bank account balance; overdraft fees can be more costly than late fees.

CHAPTER 8

Baby steps to Side Hustle Business:

Do you feel trapped in a job that you dislike?

When attempting new things , success is uncertain. Same goes for your financial commitments (rent, mortgage, auto payments, and so forth) .

However, the only options are to plunge into something new without a safety net or to accept your existing condition. There is another path to increased money and satisfaction. You may want to start a second business!

The Pain of Being Stuck

There is nothing more infuriating than being stuck.

You know where you want to go, but the actual measures to get there are hazy. It's as though you're peering across a chasm, unsure of how to get to the other side.

Whether you're not up for leaping over and testing if you can fly, running a side hustle enables you to construct a bridge methodically. It moves you closer to the direction you want to take your career—without exposing you to as much financial danger.

Why It's a Good Idea to Start a Side Hustle

Convincing oneself to work the additional hours required to start a side hustle might be difficult. Your day work already occupies a significant portion of your leisure time, and there are always friends, family, and interests to consider.

Think about this: investing in a side business today will enable you to advance to a more meaningful (and financially rewarding) level in your work life. While it does need some work and patience upfront, the result is well worth it.

Side business may or may not be a full-time job, additional cash from it solves more financial issues. You may change jobs for a lower-paying but less stressful one without losing your lifestyle. You might invest or save for retirement.

Also, side hustles allow you to test your company ideas in the real world and get crucial feedback from the market... before going "all in" and quitting your present job.

Almost everyone, with the correct technique, can utilize side hustles to supplement their income and position themselves for advancement in their employment.

How to get started right now:

1. Identify Your "Why"

Why would you want to invest the time and effort necessary to establish a side hustle? Many people do not ask this question until it's too late — when they're overwhelmed by the responsibilities of their new enterprise while juggling their day job.

Before launching your side business, it's ok to set your goals.

Are you looking for a way to increase your existing income? Or do you want to start something that will ultimately replace your present source of income and develop into a new career?

Take some time to consider your final destination. Successful side hustles result in increased income and opportunities... Nevertheless, how do you intend to spend your cash?

Knowing this information in advance, helps define your side hustle ideas and your approach to them.

My former employment was in a completely different sector from the one in which I want to work. I was well aware that my ultimate goal was to become a full-time novelist. As a result, I picked side hustles that blended internet marketing and writing to serve customers, enhance my talents, and progress toward that objective. The side hustles served as a springboard.

2. Identify a Possibility for a Side Hustle

One of the most frequent (and catastrophic) errors is to launch a side hustle solely based on your enthusiasm. It's an excellent way to begin a new activity... nevertheless, it may not be lucrative. It may not develop into a company.

Is there another way?

Begin by compiling a list of your interests. Then create another list of products/services you may supply for which people will pay. The intersection of these two areas provides rich ground for side hustle ideas!

There is also no need to come up with a unique concept. The overwhelming majority of successful firms began by enhancing or reinventing existing products/services.

You only need to choose a concept in which you may use your abilities to create something unique. Which one component of your version of the model (it just takes one!) can you accomplish better or differently than others?

Do a few weeks' worth of research, but avoid agonizing excessively over this issue. We are going to start your side business cheaply, so it won't be a big problem if the first concept fails.

3. **Validate Your Idea as Soon as Possible—and Maintain a Low Overhead**

Having a gut that your side business will succeed is insufficient. Hunches do not justify months spent developing a product without first selling anything. You don't want to spend your efforts on something that no one wants. That is horrible.

The only way to be sure you are not wasting time is to get your first client as quickly as possible. Once you have shown to yourself that others will buy into your concept, it's much simpler to remain motivated and identify areas for improvement.

Therefore, get started immediately. There is no need to spend more than $100 and a week or two to test the market and build from there.

Consider the minimal requirements for acquiring your first paying customer/client.

You will need the following:

- Something to sell,

- a willing customer, and

- a method of payment

That is all!

It's easy to get sucked into a world of business cards, flashy websites, and office rentals. However, you are not required to at this stage.

What if, instead of investing in an expensive website, you contacted a few local businesses? What if you could use your current relationships to get a customer and begin building your portfolio? This lean start-up strategy will have you earning money and receiving real-world feedback as quickly as possible – two critical components of a successful side hustle!

The bottom line is to do everything possible to prevent wasting significant amounts of time and money before determining if anything works. That way, if something does not work, it is less of a headache to go on to another concept.

4. Dedicate Time to Developing Your Side Hustle

This may be excruciating. Your life is already jam-packed with job responsibilities, and you want to make time for yourself, friends, and family. However, you'll need to find those additional hours elsewhere.

How much of your time has been lawfully reserved?

How much are you squandering?

The typical American, according to Nielsen, watch roughly five hours of television every day. That is almost a full-time job! Consider what you might accomplish if you cut that time in half and used it instead on a new venture. Things like television, online browsing, and social media are often considered low-hanging fruit. They are often the largest time wasters. Eliminate them, and you may be surprised at how much free time you discover.

If you avoid such items already and yet have a full schedule, things get more difficult, but not impossible. That is when you must examine your hobbies and social schedule critically.

Allow yourself the time you need to keep healthy (eating correctly, exercising, and sleeping enough). Working 24 hours a day to get something going is pointless if you collapse a few months later due to a breakdown in your physique. Bear in mind what Teddy Roosevelt said: "Do the best you can with what you have under the circumstances." 30 minutes or an hour a day is much superior to doing nothing. Time will pass anyhow. The sooner you begin, the sooner your hustle will take off.

5. Maximize Every Opportunity

According to a Gallup poll, 87 percent of workers are disengaged at work.

 You owe it to yourself not to be one of them. Particularly when you're pursuing a side business!

Your time is just too valuable. Working around a day job means you'll never have enough of what you desire—at least not until you decide to pursue your hustle full-time. That is why it is critical to maximizing every minute.

Set aside a set portion of your day for side hustle employment. Schedule time for your side business on your calendar just like you would for a doctor's appointment or a meeting with your most valued customer. Then, daily, keep those appointments.

Doing this first thing in the morning, before other commitments interfere, is a simple method to ensure that this task gets done (it works for me). However, if you like to hustle immediately after work or late at night, more power to you! Whatever works regularly for you is the best option.

When you're at work, strive to create the finest possible workplace. Close the door. Switch off your phone. Disconnect from social media. Make every effort to generate targeted output, and your hustling will pay off more quickly.

6. **Allow Your Side Hustle to Expand**

If you put in the effort and follow the procedures above, there is a strong probability that your side hustle may begin to generate significant revenue.

While your financial account will expand, your duties will increase proportionately. Whereas initially you just had to consider what to give a consumer, you now had to consider order fulfillment, invoicing, and customer care.

If you continue to do everything yourself, you run the risk of becoming a victim of your success. You work your day job and devote all of your spare time to maintaining your difficult side enterprise.

Without assistance, you, like everyone else, will run into the 24/7 time limit. Your expanding company comes to a halt because you lack the time or energy to expand.

Therefore, do not be frightened to seek assistance! Use part of the revenue and reinvest it in your side business, for example things like outsourcing, better tools, and tax preparation. Purchase some time and sanity for yourself while ensuring that your hustle continues to grow.

Maintain this pace, and you'll ultimately reach a point when you must decide whether to pursue your hustle full-time or maintain your day job.

Create a continuous revenue stream as you learn new skills, build relationships, and verify company ideas: starting a side hustle.

It takes time and commitment, but practically anybody can do this with the appropriate mindset and constant effort.

Even if you just have an hour a day to spare, the effects compound exponentially after a few months!

If you're a long way from your career goals, you don't have to confront your supervisor or quit.

CHAPTER

9

Thing your Neighbourhood millionaire Won't Tell You

There are approximately 3,000,000 millionaires in the United States today. And there are over 300,000,000 Americans, according to the most recent Census data, this indicates that approximately one in every hundred is a millionaire.

This means that you know someone who is a millionaire, and you almost certainly live within a stone's throw of additional millionaires you do not know.

Many millionaires have distinct habits. Characteristics that contribute to their success.

Key secrets that your neighbourhood millionaire isn't telling you.

1. Start early and Don't Make Mistakes

Many millionaires start young. It is easier to get started when you are younger. Furthermore, the earlier you start, the longer you have to watch your money grow over time. Consider this: the amount you must invest each year to reach $1,000,000 by the age of 62 is:

Starting at 25 gives you ten years more than starting at 35. You can argue all you want about the rate of return, but younger is always better than older.

This includes avoiding student loan and creditcard debt, as well as staying out of financial difficulties. Increased costs with reduced income, unemployment, gambling, poor money management, lack of money communication skills, and relying on a windfall are some of the most typical reasons for debt and financial difficulties.

You're already on par with your rich neighbour if you keep to a balanced budget and start early. Remember to prioritize your financial life.

2. Do Not Relocate or Get Divorced

 Moving and divorce are two of the most expensive aspects of life.

To begin, moving may be necessary, and it does not have to be costly. However, it is for many people. The expense of hiring movers alone can go into the $1,000s of dollars, so the more you do it, the more expensive it becomes. Second, when you are selling your house, the transaction charges are exorbitant. The more you do it, the less profit you make.

Moving can be beneficial if you are getting a better, higher-paying job or moving closer to work to save money. Just keep in mind that frequent traveling is a constant drain on your finances.

If you own a property, moving is EXPENSIVE. The math puts renting on par with buying a home unless you move frequently, in which case renting makes sense.

More on the issue of divorce. Divorce is one of the most significant wealth killers in America. Can it be avoided? No, not always.

Divorce is never the result of a lack of money; it is the result of a failure to work together with money.

Keep in mind that divorce ruins wealth. That's why your millionaire neighbour has most likely been married for a long time.

3. Invest Gradually Over Time Aside from starting young, you should also invest gradually over time. I'm not talking about dollar-cost average when investing, but start investing early and keep investing throughout your life.

This is the power of compound interest in action. As indicated in #1, the later you start, the more you have to invest to receive the same return.

Most Americans' wealth is in their homes, which they have paid off over time, or in their retirement savings, which they have painstakingly built up over time.

So, if you want to be like your rich neighbour, start on time and keep doing so regularly.

4. Establish Multiple Income Streams

Your millionaire neighbour most likely did not get there by simply doing their job. millionaires have a side business or multiple income streams. It is rare for a single-income family to achieve millionaire status. Especially when both couple worked daily. However, the better approach to making a million dollars is to work a salaried job as well as a side hustle or have some form of entrepreneurial enterprise.

By creating many income streams, you will not only build a safety net for yourself as you work toward your goals, but you can also reap the benefits of multiple income streams, particularly if some are more passive than others.

typical myths about millionaires that you should avoid if you want to become wealthy:

Myth #1: Most millionaires inherited their wealth . Only 20% of millionaires inherited their wealth. Next time you think it's impossible to make it to the million-dollar mark, remember that 80 percent of people who have done it have done so on their own (yes, you could argue that there are a lot of socio-economic factors that helped, from how they were raised to where they were born, but just because a path is more difficult doesn't make it impossible).

Myth #2: Millionaires Drive Expensive Automobiles

Daniel Mac, who chases high-end luxury car drivers in a mall and asks them "what do you do for a living," is one of my favourite TikTok channels right now. It's great to hear the responses, but it may give you the impression that the rich drive flashy automobiles.

The statistics just do not support this. According to experts, 61 percent of persons earning more than $250,000 per year drive Toyotas, Hondas, or Fords.

The following are the ten most popular automobile manufacturers among millionaires (in order of popularity):

- Toyota

- Honda

- Ford

- BMW

- Chevrolet

- Lexus

- Nissan

- Subaru

- Dodge

- Mercedes

Myth #3: Higher taxes prevent millionaires from becoming millionaires.

The idea of taxing the wealthy because 1) they dislike paying taxes in general, and 2) they do not want their dreams destroyed.

However, the truth is that taxes do not stop someone from becoming a millionaire. Taxes, on the other hand, are not a major concern for most billionaires, particularly throughout the wealth-building stages of their lives. Remember that taxes are deducted from net income, and most millionaires are only concerned with increasing that figure.

CHAPTER

10

Stop Living above Your Means

Some signs of spending too much.

It's difficult to understand why you are living above your means.

Most persons ignore their reality and continue doing what they have always done.

2. **You don't have any money in an emergency.**

Because, well, it is an emergency. If you have an unexpected bill or emergency, your only options are to charge it, take out another loan, or go deeper into your overdraft. When you run out of money five days before your next Paycheck, you shouldn't touch your emergency fund.

An emergency fund is useful for situations such as your car breaking down in the middle of nowhere, needing immediate dental care, or losing your job. They could be as low as $100, but they're more likely to cost $1000 or more.

Few of us can put together $1000 from our paychecks, which is why you need an emergency fund set aside solely for emergencies. It prevents you from taking on more debt during a stressful period.

3. **You can't pay off your credit cards in full each month.** It's fine to use your creditcard for everyday purchases as long as you pay the balance off in full each month. You have a problem if you cannot do that.

Creditcards are so simple to use; just pull them out, make a purchase, and you're done. Until you receive your credit card bill a month later and realize you've overspent and are unable to pay it off. Then the interest begins to creep up, limiting your ability to pay off even a small portion of the balance, prompting you to use the card again the following month, and the credit card spiral begins.

4. **You have due bills**

You have reached the point where you need to rob Peter to pay Paul, deciding which bills to pay and which to ignore. The fact that you are unable to pay your regular monthly bills is a clear indication that you are living beyond your means.

5. **You're paying for overdrafts**

You are back in the black when you get paid, but within a few days, you've dipped into your overdraft, where you'll stay until the next payday.

It is a horrible feeling to look at your account balance and realize you are in the red and the negative just a few days after getting paid.

Unfortunately, it makes you want to spend more because, after all, what good is saving when you are already in debt? Do not live beyond your means; that feeling of total negativity must vanish at all costs. To symbolize living beyond your means, a woman's hands are holding open an empty grey purse.

You Don't Have Any Retirement Funds

You're preoccupied with today's expenses rather than plan for your retirement, which may be many years away. Spending too much is easy; spending less is a little more difficult. Mostly because your lifestyle and financial habits have been built around your excessive spending. It's easier to keep doing what you've always done rather than switching things up and trying something new.

What are the benefits of living within your means?

1. Make a Promise to Yourself

Promise yourself to stop living beyond your means and to be more frugal with your money. You realize you need to cut back on your spending and adjust your lifestyle to fit a more realistic financial situation. However, you can still enjoy life while living within your means; it's just a different way of life, not a bad one. You can commit to spending less in a variety of ways. Financial goals and no-spend days are two of my favourites. Goals for future spending, as well as no-spend days for the time being. If there's one thing that will bring peace and contentment to a human heart and a family, it's living within one's means.

2. Develop Budgeting Skills

A budget is an essential tool in the fight to live within your means.

Every month, your budget will help you understand how much money you have coming in and how much money you have in commitments going out. Look at your bank and credit card statements from the previous month.

List all of your expenses, including bills, automatic payments, car and transportation expenses, as well as more flexible spending such as groceries and entertainment. Add them all together, and don't be surprised if the total exceeds your monthly income. Expect something like this to happen. Because your spending last month demonstrates that, you are living beyond your means. You must now reduce your numbers and expenses to the point where you spend less than you earn.

Fastest Way To Become A Millionaire

Get Married to a Millionaire

People think this is simple and quick, but it is not. It is easier and faster than starting a business, growing it, and earning money on your own, but you cannot marry a millionaire overnight.

First, you must identify some millionaires. Where do you look for them? Fortunately, much of the information available online is now simple and quick. Compiled a list of the top ten websites for finding a sugar daddy. Many of these sites also have pages for those looking for sugar mamas — there is no discrimination here. Some of these arrangements are expected to be superficial and short-lived, but many relationships begin this way. It all depends on your ability to persuade.

That being said, it is understood that your physical beauty will play a role in your power. You must be beautiful to marry and support a wealthy person. Consider it an investment in your future if it involves plastic surgery and a few hours a day at the gym. Keep in mind that many millionaires are astute and may request that you sign a prenuptial agreement, which is only fair. You can only live the lifestyle of the rich and famous in these arrangements if you are married to the person and keep your end of the bargain (eg., no eating chips and donuts, and no cheating with someone young and attractive).

2. Hazard

This is commonly accomplished by purchasing lottery tickets, and it is one of the quickest ways to become a millionaire. It's almost instantaneous — but it's not easy. When a jackpot grows large, many people buy extra tickets in the hope of increasing their chances of winning. Yes, it does. However, the difference is so small that it is statistically insignificant. Consider your chances of winning to be like grass blades on a football field. You double your chances if you get two blades.

They are, however, still infinitesimal. Some people win a lot of money in casinos. Most people, however, do not. Slot machines are popular because everyone enjoys seeing a single pay-out, all those coins spilling out, lights flashing, and sound effects. However, the chances of winning are slim. The chances of someone winning are high; however, the chances of it being you are low. If you want to win at gambling, the best bet is to play a game that requires some strategy, such as blackjack or poker. To become a millionaire, however, you must be extremely talented and win numerous times.

3. Create Something

The catch is that it has to be something that people want. It does not need to be good or useful; it simply needs to be popular. Do you recall Cabbage Patch Kids? Consider 25 inventions that earned their creators millions of dollars. People who stayed up too late thinking outside the box most likely conceived some of these ideas. Therefore, that could be a step in the right direction. If this were the case, inventing something would be one of the best ways to become a millionaire.

4. Invest in a successful Business.

This is similar to having a 401(k), but on a larger scale. With a 401(k), you choose your level of risk, and someone else decides where your money will be invested. You usually make money, though not always a million dollars. To invest a million dollars, you must put a lot of money into a company and expect big returns. True, you could have made a million dollars by purchasing a few shares of the original AT&T stock, but you'd have had to wait a long time — nearly a century.

Look for investment opportunities online, court smart people with ideas but no money, a la Shark Tank, or fund your cousin's empanada truck — the format doesn't matter; the only thing that matters is that they succeed. In addition, that they return your money to you.

I'm not sure what this is, other than the fact that people claim to be getting rich off of it. Is it genuine? Nobody knows. We are not sure if investing in Bitcoin will make you a millionaire, but if it does, it'll be as simple as a few mouse clicks.

6. Become Famous

It makes no difference how or why, for better or worse, most famous people have more money than the average Joe. Is it true that famous people are famous because they have money? Sometimes. And here's the conundrum: if being famous makes you rich, but you can't get famous without money, how will you ever get there?

Being born a Kardashian or Hilton indeed makes things easier. Then you can have cosmetic surgery to achieve the beauty that God withheld from you at birth, and you will be on your way. Because photographers enjoy photographing beautiful people doing exciting things such as relaxing on a yacht. We will go over a few ideas for how to become famous.

Make it big on YouTube.

Obtain a spot on reality television shows such as The Bachelor.

Make friends with celebrities.

Make a career as an actor or singer.

Become a successful athlete.

Run for office and get elected.

Do something out of the ordinary to catch everyone's

attention.

7. Practise Aggressive savings

A couple of years ago, CNBC ran a story about a couple who saved enough money in four years to retire at the age of 43. Sounds impossible, doesn't it?

It's worth noting that they had always been good savers and had a lot of money in their 401(k) at the time they launched their plan (k). They also determined that they — and their two children — could live on $24,000 per year after analyzing their lifestyle and expenses. (!)

A story about a family like this can always be found in a magazine on the grocery checkout rack. They clip coupons and eat for $5 per week, get their clothes from dumpsters, and watch TV through the windows of their neighbors for entertainment. Do you truly want to become a millionaire in this manner? Are the pain and humiliation worth it?

Assume you embarked on a reasonable plan in which you diligently saved for 20 years and eventually amassed a million dollars. In the United States, the median household income is $56,516. With no raises, you could earn a million dollars in 20 years at this salary. But you lack the necessary funds. Because you had no choice but to live. So a million dollars is more than a figure on a piece of paper. It's a feeling of liberation, excitement, and enjoyment.

8. Put in the effort

We put this one last because it's the least enjoyable and the most difficult way to become a millionaire. The chances of success are higher than those of playing the lottery, and the return on investment is more satisfying. But it is, of course, difficult. two things but do not work hard, you will most likely not get there.

Indeed, you can sometimes get something for nothing. But not always. And when you do get something for free, it's frequently an illusion, or it's outright bad or dangerous. So be cautious. Also, be astute.

These are our top eight methods for becoming a millionaire. We didn't include anything illegal. Those strategies do occasionally work, but we don't believe they're worth the risk.

www.ingramcontent.com/pod-product-compliance
Lightning Source LLC
Chambersburg PA
CBHW031222160726
47992CB00006B/2860